ALL THE DIFFERENT DARKNESSES

GILL HORITZ

Published by Cinnamon Press
Meirion House
Tanygrisiau
Blaenau Ffestiniog
Gwynedd, LL41 3SU
www.cinnamonpress.com

The right of Gill Horitz to be identified as author of this work has been asserted by her in accordance with the Copyright, Designs and Patent Act, 1988. Copyright © 2018 Gill Horitz.
ISBN: 978-1-78864-039-8
British Library Cataloguing in Publication Data. A CIP record for this book can be obtained from the British Library.
All rights reserved. No part of this publication may be reproduced, stored in a retrieval system, or transmitted in any form or by any means, electronic, mechanical, photocopying, recording or otherwise without the prior written permission of the publishers. This book may not be lent, hired out, resold or otherwise disposed of by way of trade in any form of binding or cover other than that in which it is published, without the prior consent of the publishers.
Designed and typeset in Palatino by Cinnamon Press.
Cover design by Jan Fortune. Printed in Poland
Cinnamon Press is represented in the UK by Inpress Ltd and in Wales by the Welsh Books Council

Acknowledgements

Thanks to the editors of the following publications, in which some of the poems have appeared, sometimes as earlier versions: *Ink, Sweat & Tears, Words for the Wild, Mslexia, Smiths Knoll, Seven* (Impulse Press), *New Forest Poetry Anthology, Tears in the Fence, Poetry School.*

Special thanks to long-term writing companions, Wendy Wharam, and Tony Horitz and to members of Paul Hyland's Poetry in Progress seminar group whose invaluable comments have contributed to the development of many of the poems.

Contents

All the different darknesses of the world	7
His Own Yard	8
Fear of Being Forgotten	9
Things Recovered from a Shipwreck	10
But an Object Lying in Wait	11
Beyond the Feel of Things	12
Beaker Bowl	13
My Exact Dread	14
Sweetheart, Come	15
Ladybirds	16
After the Accident	17
Left to Her Own Devices	18
Woolf's Dream	19
What is worse	20
Murmuration	21
Dealing with the Unthinkable	22
Because Glasses Don't Fit in Snorkel Masks	23
Strange Matter	24
What Has To Be Broached	25
Last Thing Sunday Night	26
Visiting my Mother in a Rest Home	27
A Father, What He Amounts To	28
Remembering Tortilla Flat	29
Art	30
Francis Bacon at my Granddaughter's 21st	31
Mary's Children	32
Living Signs	33
Seventy	34
Budapest	35
The Living Room	36
What Lies in the Winter Wood	37

For Annie and Muriel,
Sarah, Karina, Daniel
and Tony

All the different darknesses

All the different darknesses of the world

and one such dark was formed from shadows
reaching as far in as the bedside mat
which sat like a little island on the parquet floor
where we undressed. From the top bunk I looked down
on our earrings signaling in the lamplight, red beads
to crystals, and when we turned our pages
the frame gave little shudders, not frighteningly
but in the way of a reminder: what is granted,
take it, full force. And when my granddaughter
leaned out to scoop air in quick beating motions,
another kind of dark opened in me. Of forgetting
these invisible things: the two of us
in a small boat and the sun not far off.

His Own Yard

I remember thinking the travellers on the Overground
would think nothing of five figures in a yard
at the back of homes but we were there
and it was us and in the quiet between trains
there were poppies where they'd not been
the night before and what remained of a rose
trying to begin again and when he went in
to put on the kettle the memory of the morning
was beginning to form and when he called
breakfast's ready I watched my son walking
on the hard earth of his own yard
and how he got there part of the past
still moving through me

Fear of Being Forgotten

Towards the end of winter,
the bedroom chest groans
when spring wakes the grain.

Inside, a mother's hair,
the thickest brown, waiting
to be stroked or spoken about.

Each spring more easing of wood.
Each spring becomes the last
if no-one comes, no-one thinks to look.

Things Recovered from a Shipwreck

Fruit Forks
Piano Keys
Chessmen

someone's belongings
sought after, brought up
into the dry world to live

behind glass a half life
in which they exact nothing
except their own shape,

the names of things
on small white cards
stand like guards
against their past

yet nothing so recoverable
from the three drowned women
as their own names brimming
with the selves they might have been

Eliza Peirce
Mary Peirce
Amy Paul

But an Object Lying in Wait

holds its own life in the shape it makes,
the way my grandmother's coat
appeared at the back of a drawer
where it hadn't been before,
and I said, let me hold it, quickly!

It took me in its arms and we fell back
onto the bed, and from out the cloth
the exact smell of her blue crepe came,
as though she might breathe again
and I would remember more and more.

Beyond the Feel of Things

Two Mauser bullets, a stretch of wire
from fields at Redan Ridge,
one postcard, stamped 1914,
from James to Lizzie Roberts,
'We're moving tomorrow
but I can't say where.
Yours ever.'

          And ever since, what's left
keeps turning up, the things
they touched. However hard we try
we never reach beyond the feel
of things; never the moment –
head open to the sky - his thoughts
flocked away through greying light.

Beaker Bowl

Of its whereabouts, this bowl
knows nothing and is unknown
to most of the world except
when I lean over the ledge where it lives

half-lit under glass, and see myself fallen
into the bowl's interior dark, the same
dark opening my mother's mouth made
waiting for language to fill up.

My Exact Dread

Waking in the dark
I found my exact dread:

a bird presiding
at the foot of the bed, one eye

so deep in a yellow ring,
it seemed he saw what I'd been thinking

lately, about death being round
the corner, and how

I hold company still
with the kind of thoughts

that come in rooms
where darkness always lives

in dark. Advancing towards me,
his feet felt tender

as if his wise arriving
might bring an end to fear,

and I could make a choice - cry out
or stay and watch his black beak open.

Sweetheart, Come

This room won't let me out. Today
I measured our farmyard in it.
Twenty chickens would fit
or our bed, if it was our home.
But there's no weather, no window.
The doctor says if one word could save me,
what would it be? Then this paper arrived
to keep me company. And a pencil under the bed.

My hand and this wand set out to fetch you,
spelling *komm komm komm* over and over,
covering the distance between us
until half way down the page *komm*
becomes a boat with a mast at the bow
and we're lying on deck, side by side with bent knees.
In the centre is the o, the engine
beating like my heart will when you fetch me.

Ladybirds

You must believe me. Four ladybirds
on the dressing table in their defined order,
their number of spots reliable as time
telling me the safe hour
to go out.

I went to the park. Red shoes
under a rose bush striking a pose
to indicate north.

I went in that direction because I had to
and when I came home, the ladybirds
were dead and my pillow
crushed.

After the Accident

Dawn outside in the dark-edged garden
and she's feeling her way in the kitchen

noticing how many crusts and rinds left
on the worktop lie in the form of questions

about whose fault it should best be:
the ice, the clock, the four-by-four,

or the resistance in her mind
to believe this once it wasn't hers,

though blame breathes in her.
Objects with their motives,

pretending innocence: callous
metal pinioning her legs,

the glove compartment recklessly
opening itself to the cruel world.

Left to Her Own Devices

That zone, never properly mapped
between closed curtains and glass,

a last resort for skulking children
left to their own devices after dark.

Any lost place will do when a girl's
not missed by her own flesh and blood.

She pulled her toes in fast. The look
on the girl's face staring in, still recalled,

and her voice through the glass
daring her to come, ready or not.

Woolf's Dream

I'm at the window
watching the road
travelling in the wrong direction.

I see nothing bright or specific
just a continuous blankness
my duty must resolve

with a new nib,
to enclose everything
until the paper wears thin.

Behind me, my diaries
stacked to a height
of considerable risk,

every outing and encounter
contained, everything
I need never say again

on the point of collapse.
It's all done. Each trumped
argument, everything complete.

The river, losing its chalky blue light
as soon as someone slips in.

What is worse

than when a terribly thin woman
steps through the bedroom wall
and points the blade tips of her eyes
in my direction with so much ungenerous
intention I say nothing but think
fearful thoughts about how to call out
the word *help* into the room but even one
helpful syllable refuses to be uttered, holed-up
at the back of my throat where nothing
but air enters and leaves in bellowfulls until the sound
of a cranked car starts in my windpipe, the sound
of stones grinding through the ages a dream takes,
the sound of fear trying to call in its own voice?

Murmuration

We were in the reed beds
waiting for starlings
when the phone rang
and her voice was blown
by the blue air into my ear,
speaking about the past
which wouldn't leave her,
a kind of punishment,
she was saying, to be unknown
or alone, the wind
made it hard to hear.

I was still listening at four-thirty
when the air chilled, fell inert
as birds appeared
on the same wavelength
as dusk, accumulating
in swathes, each one
dependent on the nearest.

If she could see what starlings
make of themselves, bound
by their own instinct.

Dealing with the Unthinkable

Where best consigned?
Held under guard in a cavity
of breast bone confined
all night incommunicado
the thought whacked full pelt
on its back   wings strapped flat
eyes blacked out
by her mind veering north
where nothing is yet
endangered a bearable
steadying light stays the arrival
of Friday where the inexpressible
waits until the last moment possible
when the thought gets loose
and becomes
thinkable

Because Glasses Don't Fit in Snorkel Masks

The price was fifty dollars a head.
Last thing I said before we slid out
the boat's stern, *Take care!*

I wanted to shout *Live*!
to my last child about to dance
over coral in the Pacific.

Thirty snorkellers partying
and me on the edge, half blind
with a strapped on eye

and my glasses folded dryly
in the boat, me on the edge
of voices running into each other

and no telling rocks from heads.
Unmendable moment
through which his white heels

fell like pears sliced into the arms
of coral and me his mother
with not enough breath left

to throw his lifebelt name.
Seconds later, as though
from the future in which

we'll separate as air
from water, he waved from a rock,
and my breath filled his name.

Strange Matter

Six of us spread along the beach
finding our own way to scatter ash.

Hinged shells filled and thrown;
like casting seed or feeding hens.
No two ways the same.

Wind whips her ash
into flames over water, blowing
into our mouths, and some
into the shallows.

She would have loved that last sight
of herself, my scientist mother, bone
pinheads starring in their new element.

What Has To Be Broached

We're in the garden
facing each other
in front of a vine.

As we chat
in little bursts
about the mildew,

a wind comes up
after a spell of stillness,
and blows her hair.

If I had courage
I would say, *your hair
that once I once plaited!*

and forget what's to be
broached. But I begin
one word after another,

the way stones
were laid to make a path
from our house
into the cold world.

Last Thing Sunday Night

Iron last from a cobbler's corner,
from the shoe-horn days of
caring for family hide. Hoicked from
the back pantry by my Dad
last thing Sunday night.

Kneeling on the kitchen floor,
he laid shoes paired
on newspaper like dead rabbits,
creamed their creases,
mysteriously housed iron
feet in the invisible air
of our footwear.

The closest we came, our family's
shoes on the kitchen floor, with him
hammering home Blakeys, the shape
of kidneys, dabbing saliva
on our worn down heels,
the closest we came
to kisses.

Visiting my Mother in a Rest Home

No-one moves or speaks.
Six hundred years
power the air as they wait
held by the soft chair arms, weight
bone-light on the draylon.

She and I play scrabble
on the table shine, invent
codes while Vera chafes
fire in Wally's lap. Only I notice
her mount his chair arm,
her old roan back in Rahinnane
the pair of them heads back
eyes tight shut, flying
to the body's far reaches
in the deathly lounge
where I thought nothing
moved all day except their eyes.

When he died, Vera
had no knowing who
would be next in his chair.
The sight of its wings
set her rocking, the same
rhythm as she forgot
and forgot and bent over
the table, tongued a trail
across old mahogany,
as though tasting a lover's skin.

A Father, What He Amounts To

Magnolia buds presented
themselves differently,
they uplifted as though nothing
could compel death to reach inside
their grey skin.

The January light was more
notable when you and I went back
for his belongings to the room
where he died.

His climbing boots were paired
neatly as he and I had never been,
and his torn denims left
on the chair back waited
to be disposed of.

When you unhooked the keys
from his belt, it wasn't stealing.
Nothing could unlock
what he still owed.

He didn't even wait, the man
we drove to reach, but died alone
under a yellow counterpane.

Remembering Tortilla Flat

The first thing I woke to was the rook
tacked to Danny's doorpost.
Weighing up its meaning
I think of the past we talk about
too much, the rose of Castile,
remembering the house, sweet families
under the long grass
where lay a fallen gavel
turned iron dark
and a yard full
of what he called
a memorable grey calm
waiting to be whipped up,
and men on high backs,
hurrying us along.

Through the door screen
roosters and crows whirl
in the dust bowl.
And the lone man
carrying faith
in his foolish heart
is never free from this,
looped against the barbed wire
by his shoe strap.

I was sixteen when I
came across Danny
and the trance of Monterey
stays at the back of my mind:
the horizon - what you hope for,
the corrugated iron roof — the shape you want
for the rest of your life.

Art

Punters glance with barbs
at her confessional. What Tracey calls
a sweet moment in history.
But where is compassion? On that bed
she almost died of thirst. Easy to smirk
at loneliness. Wordsworth they love,
daffodils much easier on the inward eye
than an enchantment of stained cotton and drecks,
all the fallen bits of her, slippers, tissues,
gin culled into a metaphor of things,
a precise configuration about
the death of then. What was meant
was missed. So what happens next?

Someone else guiding us in.
Other versions of the same unease.

Francis Bacon at my Granddaughter's 21st

I will him to appear at her door, framed
against the outer darkness, the man
up close, straight from the back
of her mind where he hangs out, noisy
with sayings she likes the sound of.

From room to room he'll roam,
pour champagne, his lips
slouched in her direction,
a white-jowled knowing look.

Next day, she draws
her way across a white expanse,
a stream of consciousness, saying
and unsaying—*here I come*.

Mary's Children

Mary's children are born
in the barn. Labour is life's work
and the womb weighs a ton.

She handles the chain tackle
easy as a bell pull. They face
the way she puts them.
Visitors bend and peer,
put their fingers into fissures
and declare.

It takes time. Her feet paddle
in dust all week. What emerges
depends on the quality of light
and the mother's own memory.

Sometimes a horse craves
the rider in its own way.
Mary has no say.
This is not delinquency —
children have their way to be.

They're my children, Mary laughs
when they leave. *You love them to go.*

But stone isn't flesh
nor do you want it so.

Living Signs

At night waiting in the dark
I begin to think of a door
half open on the unlived years
already coming in. Dawns

beginning earlier and earlier
and more welcome than before.
A brilliance fills the bedside glass
half full the more I look this spring

and things appear never before seen
or heard. Something is going on
with time. A small thud in my chest
going hurry, hurry.

I thought I was grown up
but now I expect more
from the way my mind
reassembles living signs.

Colours, folds in nature,
an ordinary lapwing.

Seventy

At night she holds
different parts of herself
into one consolable shape,

the various girls she once was,
wrestling each other
in her mind, some willing

to be remembered, some
preferring to be passed over
or never found: that girl,

alone in Miller's Woods
talking to no-one about the feverish
blue of the flowers, didn't know

her own capacity, even
the next street was too far;
and the other girl

but the same, high-skipping
down the path to Ann Smith's door,
arousal in her heart:

*life is a length of years
and I have lived six…*

Now, one of the last, remembering
herself as she is, not counting
under her breath.

Budapest

Like being summoned I hurry to the window
and in the one tree, so close
it almost touches the glass - the bird,

dove-grey in early light, its little mouth
turning the air with a five-boned tongue,
into a song. And as it sings, along the street

to right and left, the windows gleam and quiver,
and the roofs of the parked cars reflect
its shivery brilliance. Under my feet

the parquet vibrates, and the whole house
moves as the nameless bird returns to earth
what keeps getting lost, a particular thing

to belong to, song, very old and invisible,
which brings to mind every morning, a reminder
of something small but expressible.

The Living Room

You sit with the sun pouring in
as though alone in a glade
by a stream listening to birds
inside a blackthorn bush.

You think about the undergrowth
where they live their guarded lives
and inside your head ask
one of the birds, could I come in?

You wake to the consolation
of the room, your hand
on a pile of books,
and think, perhaps I can.

What Lies in the Winter Wood

End of day, end of year—and she's thinking what's next,
head against the pane and the wind slamming the gate.

When she looks up, the trees are moving through the half-light
towards her, through snow piled over the vanished road.
Not a single thought holds her back.
All the meanings held by the trees she remembers,
and how their barks can unroll and be written upon.
No ordinary wood moves like this, and time is short.

Through the holly tunnels she sings a low song to the owl
and the night leans down, savouring her wintry breath.
What will I take from this? she thinks, looking back
as the moon hurries her along. To believe just once
that such a place exists, the imaginary heart
where everything worth moving towards lies.

Notes:

Beaker Bowl
This poem is a response to the black pottery of a Neolithic pot on display in Dorchester Museum.

Things Recovered From a Shipwreck
This poem refers to three women who drowned in the wreck of the Halsewell which sank off the Purbeck coast in 1786. Some artefacts are on display in Dorchester Museum.

Sweetheart, Come
This poem is inspired by a letter written in 1923 but never sent, from Emma Hauck, in Weisloch Asylum, to her husband, composed entirely of the word 'komm' written repeatedly across the page.

Art
This poem refers to 'My Bed' by Tracey Emin

Mary's Children
Mary Spencer Watson, Dorset Sculptor, 1914 — 2006